MW00884361

BEST BU __

THE HOW TO OF NEGOTIATING YOUR NEXT NEW OR USED CAR OR TRUCK

Negotiate your best lease, finance or cash deal

in less than 30 minutes

without confrontation

by knowing how a dealership works.

BURL JOHNSON

Table of Contents

BEST BUYER BOOK OF NEGOTIATING YOUR NEXT NEW OR USED CAR OR TRUCK

Copyright 2017 by Burl Johnson

Published by Sydalex Publishing

First Printing: March 2017

First Edition: March 2017

To my two wonderful kids, Sydney and Alex, who make everything worthwhile.

PREFACE

There is no denying that going to buy a car is one of the more stressful shopping experiences you will have. It's that way for your salesperson too, for different reasons. The information in this book will give you everything you need to buy a car in less than 30 minutes at the dealer, instead of the usual 4 hours, and when you drive away in your new car, you won't feel like you paid too much, and you and your salesperson won't feel so stressed out.

This book is not about what car or truck to buy. That is determined by your wants and needs. What this book is about, it's how auto dealers make their money off you, the consumer. You may shop for weeks for the best price, and you may get it, but the real profit for the dealer comes after you say yes.

I didn't learn this stuff off a video, reading a book, or working a stint as a salesman for a few months. This is what I have learned and practiced every day. I know it can help you save money, and feel good about whatever it is you buy. I retired from the car business after 28 years. Being a salesman selling

40 cars a month, then a sales manager, and a general sales manager, I think makes me qualified to let you in on the inside.

I wanted to make this a quick learn, you don't need to read a 300-page book to get the information. It's laid out so you can read the whole thing if you want, but categorized also to tell you only what you need to know.

I promise that the information will save you hundreds, if not thousands on your next auto purchase, and maybe tens of thousands over the course of a lifetime. Look at it this way. If you can read it in a couple of hours and save a few hundred bucks, that's not too bad. But if you save $5000 on just one purchase, that's a very good return.

Just laying a copy of this book on your car seat when they do the trade appraisal will save you money. Dealers do not like an informed buyer. And yes, we do go through your car on appraisals. If the appraiser thinks you have done your research, they will give you a much larger first offer on your car. And the sales desk will not start the deal so high. I know, that's what I did.

You may not be in the market right now, but you will be. You never know when you need to buy a car, and this insider way of doing business, hasn't changed in 30 years.

CHAPTER 1
WHERE TO START

Let's briefly cover how you shop for a car before we get into the nuts and bolts, because how it starts does have an impact on your deal. You need a car, dealerships have cars, we now have a buyer and a seller. No matter how much everyone dances around, that's the fact. There are basically four ways to start your communication with a dealer. Let's talk about how they may impact your experience.

I want to give you some statistics about the closing ratio of buyers and where they come from. Closing ratio is how many people buy compared to how they shop.

Internet inquiries – 12%

Phone inquiries -   18%

Fresh walk in   -   20%

Referrals   -   38%

Repeat buyer   -   62%

INTERNET: An average dealer, if there is such a thing, handles from 300 to 500 internet leads a month. It's a seasonal business, so obviously some months more, some less, depending on location. That same dealer will get about 125 phone calls, 75 fresh walk-ins (didn't talk to someone first), and maybe about 50 repeat customers, or referrals that get sent in.

So unless you have "your car guy" or recommended to someone, chances are you are starting your process on the internet, and I would recommend that is what you do. This is where you have the most control, and the party with the most control, is the one who wins.

Like I said, I'm not interested in what you buy, and if you use the internet, I assume you can figure out that shopping multiple dealers for price quotes, you will be getting a realistically priced quote. As we dig in, you will find out the pitfalls and traps to look for.

Dealers will either have a BDC (Business Development Center) that handles internet leads, a specific contact person to do them, or randomly pass them out to salespeople. You will have no idea what you get when you submit a lead. It would be preferable to have a dedicated internet person as your contact, they are much better trained to handle your requests for information in a timely manner. Some salesman just don't get how it works, or have no interest, and do it just in hopes they get a lay down (an easy uniformed buyer). Most dealer websites have their staff pictures, what their position is, and contact information. If you get poor service, I suggest you contact the manager by email, and they will be more than willing to help you, much more so since you started out on the wrong foot.

The goal of the dealership, no matter how you start your communication with them, is to get you physically in the door. Then control switches to them. These people do this for a living, and a good salesperson sells you something without you even knowing you have been sold.

After you have shopped pricing, they will want to talk about your trade and how you intend to buy, finance, lease, or cash. No matter what form of method you intend to use, or have a trade, do not give this information until you have a solid price commitment in writing. I'll be talking about this throughout the book.

PHONE: There Is only one goal that the salesperson wants when talking to a prospect on the phone. To get you to come in. Give as little information as possible, and get you to come in. They take enormous amounts of training with that goal in mind, to get you to come in. The rapport they try to develop with you , starts on the phone. Internet is too anonymous and impersonal. Many salespeople have a script on their desk to follow, with a step by step plan to get information, and not give it.

Some salespeople will make lots of promises on the phone. When I first started selling cars, I presented my customers with a trade figure on their car, which was too low for them. They left. My manager saw them pulling out of the driveway and rushed to ask what happened. I told him that they wanted two thousand more for their trade, I was too green to know I had to speak to the manager before anyone left. He told me to call them up and offer them the two thousand more. Since they lived 60 miles away, I waited a couple of hours, called them up, and gave them the good news. They drove back that afternoon. When I brought the deal to my manager for him to sign, he asked me why I thought I could give them more for their trade. I reminded him of what he said, and he laughed and said he just wanted to see if I could get them back in the store, and no way they are getting more. Needless to say, they left mad. And I never did that again.

The phone is where the salesperson really tries to dig for as much info as he can from you, to be able to use it to advantage later. You will see how that all works later.

WALK-IN: This is the golden ticket on any car lot. This is why you see salespeople hanging around the lot. Especially if all the decision makers are there, husband, wife, Dad, Mom, kids, whoever. You generally have your trade with and salespeople assume everyone has a trade. This is when the salesperson starts selling themselves, build rapport, offers you coffee, balloons for the kids, and justifying why you should buy the product from them.

Of course, many times they greet someone who is looking for a specific salesperson, one they know or worked with on the phone or internet. Then you become the hot potato, no one wants to help, no money in it for them, and now you are just wasting their time.

It takes a bigger commitment to drive on the lot, and they know you are farther down the road to buying, which means maybe a sale today. I will repeat this again, but never buy on your first trip to a dealer, no matter how "Too good to be true" it seems. The exception is if you have taken the time to research price, trade, and financing options before you set foot on the lot. Still, you will always get that same deal the next time, and 90% of the time, a better deal if you do walk out and come back.

REPEAT BUYER: If this is your 2nd, 3rd, or tenth vehicle from the same salesperson, you are a repeat buyer. This is the bread and butter for a seasoned salesperson's career, and income. You obviously have been happy with the service they provided, and have trust in them. A salesperson will always hold more gross (money) on a repeat customer, than a fresh informed one. That trust comes with a price. If this is what you are, I still recommend you shop price, financing, and trade from other dealers, even though you still intend to buy from your former salesperson. As we say in the business, just to keep him honest.

REFERRAL: If you have been recommended to a salesperson, you sort of fit in the Repeat Buyer category. Your defenses are down, you have more trust just from the recommendation, and you may shop this person first, to try to save yourself some hassle and some time. Again, do your homework before you contact them.

We will cover every aspect of the buying process in the following chapters. Before we go any further, I just want to say that a dealership is a business that employs people who depend on that income to raise their families and have a good life. They deserve to make a profit, you deserve to preserve some of your hard earned money, and there is no reason it can't be a win/win for both parties. I'm not sharing this information so you can go in and make life miserable for the dealership. Dealerships are a vital part of the communities they serve, and contribute a lot to charity, provide income and employment to a bunch of supporting businesses, and pay their fair share of taxes. Even corporate owned stores leave most of the money locally. So just as you wouldn't go into your favorite restaurant and demand they sell you your meal for cost (they would spit in your food then), or get gas at the station and offer to pay them fifty cents a gallon less than what they are asking, please don't think they deserve to work for nothing. They provide a valuable service, your transportation needs, and should be compensated so they can remain in business and be there when you need them. From the outside looking in, it may seem like a bunch of crooks just trying to get your money. In reality, they are some of the hardest working, honest, and nicest people I have ever me, and that is in all the dealerships I have worked in. Believe me, when you are dealing with the customers a dealership has to face every day, I think you end up seeing the worst in people, or maybe in some, their true selves. The customers are far worse than the employees. There is an old saying in the business, "Buyers are Liars" and many times it's true. You hear it all. In fact, I think a sitcom about a dealership and all the different situations that come up would be hilarious. My advice, be yourself, be honest, be kind, and you will be treated the same. Isn't that what everyone wants?

CHAPTER 2
FINANCE, LEASE, OR PAY CASH

Let's go back to the beginning. As far back as recorded history goes, there has been negotiation. The world's oldest occupation was prostitution as we all are told. And there starts negotiation. Barter for goods and services. In fact, it probably dates back to the cave man, dinosaur bone for spear, spear for cave, cave for woman, you get the picture. Even if someone is trying to take something from you by force, you negotiate to try not to get killed in the process. In the United States, there are only a handful of goods exchange that have a long history of real negotiation. Real estate, business transactions ,court cases, and of course, auto sales. A lot of that is changing in the auto business with what they call one-price, or non-negotiating stores, but even then, there is still quite a bit of negotiating going on which I will get in to. Let's start.

First off, a car dealership is not unlike many typical retail establishments. It is split into 3 separate and distinct parts. Sales, service and parts are usually under one roof, but separated by department. Each one has one or more managers that report to a General Manager, who may or not have any ownership in the business. The trend of dealerships has gone the way of family farms. Due to the high cost of operation, the high cost of inventory and the high cost to buy one, many dealerships are now part of a dealership group, from as little as two stores, to as high as hundreds. Unless advertised that way, you would probably never even know if they are locally or corporate owned. Doesn't really matter, the business model and practices are almost identical.

You need or want a car. There is a difference. If you are a need buyer, you might have a car that quit running, needs expensive repairs, your lease is done, or a car for someone just getting their license, etc. A want buyer is someone who wants to upgrade their existing car, or treating themselves to an extra one just for fun. A salesperson will generally be more aggressive with a need buyer knowing that they are in the market now, and aren't just shopping around with time to make a decision.

Before you ever step one foot in a dealership, you need to do your homework first. On the internet. When I started selling cars and managing, there was no internet. The dealership definitely had the upper hand. No one really knew what their trades were worth, what the dealership invoice was, or what was a fair deal , nothing to compare it with. The margins (the difference between the cost and the MSRP) were much higher then, sometimes as much as 25%. Some models now are as low as 3%. Let's break down the difference between buying a new car vs a used car.

Depending on the make of car (Honda, Toyota, Ford) you are looking for, there will be anywhere from 1 to many dealerships handling the same exact cars in any given area. It's called a franchise, and their right to a certain area is protected by state law. With the internet, you can shop at hundreds of dealerships if you want, but you don't need to. Because new cars are so competitive, and the manufacturer requires a certain amount to be sold to keep the dealership in good standing, most dealerships will either advertise or internet price them with little or no profit left, just to get the sale. There are also many buying services at big box stores like Costco, Sam's Club, Credit Unions and others that make arrangements with the dealerships for their best pricing for their members. They are not the best pricing. You can do the same or often better by working directly with the dealer. There are also lots of places on the internet that you can get the invoice price of any car you are interested in. These are somewhat accurate, not always, but in no way give you what the dealership is making on any car. New cars have a lot of manufacturer incentives that never get passed on to the consumer, unlike consumer rebates and low interest offers. There are also volume incentives, holdback, CSI (survey) incentives, and more that come into the dealership as profit. I remember when I started selling cars, we were proud to say we were selling one particular car at invoice, which the customers thought meant our cost. We were still making $7500 a car on the sale. That much is rare these days, but once in a while it happens. One more thing to note about shopping for new cars, a dealership can trade with another of the same makes, and have it brought anywhere you want . It's called a dealer trade, and it happens a lot. There should be no fee to do this. Part of doing business.

Used cars are usually more profitable for the dealership to sell. They generally sit on the lot for a shorter amount of time, which would then not cost as much to floor plan (pay interest on the inventory), and since every used car is different than any other, miles, condition, color, and selection is less, they are usually priced with a fair amount of profit when it first gets to the lot, then gradually gets repriced the longer it sits. There is a lot of pressure to move used inventory quickly, as they lose value every month. A salesperson will always want to sell you the freshest used car on the lot, because they have the most profit in them. Because of the differences in used cars, it is harder to compare prices exactly, but the internet has enough of each kind to give you at least a starting point. Many dealers, and I was one, will sell used cars to customers hundreds of miles away, and ship them by truck. Many hard to find cars are sold this way. You certainly want to have a lot of trust in that dealer.

Buying a car should be fun. Your salesperson wants you to feel that way. One of the sayings in the car business is "your happiest customers are your biggest gross customer", That means you paid more than anyone else. Being on both sides, there is no reason to not make it enjoyable, and if you don't care about saving money, then go in unprepared, pay whatever they ask, have a blast, and move on. More power to you. But if you are like the majority of people, buying cars are the second biggest expense of your life, saving money is not only prudent, but it may be essential.

Let's talk first about the elephant in the room. The fact is that you may not know what you want, and the determining factor is how they feel, drive, fit in the garage, looks on you, and what your friends think. I would want to know those things too. Here's the problem. Once you walk into a dealership, you are greeted by a salesperson, who now claims right to you if you ever come back. If they are very good at what they do, you might be driving a car home that day without doing your homework, and spending much more than you should. Or they might be horrible to work with, and if you go back there, are stuck with them which will make your whole buying experience horrible. If you can, take the time to drive out of your area, find a dealership that carries the same product line, and do your driving there. You will want to buy local if you can, it helps the local economy, and having people know you when you come in for service is nice for you. If you have friends who own the same car, ask to drive theirs, or go to the dealership when they are closed to do a bit of window shopping. Try to narrow the search to three or less models, any more and you may just give up trying to get a deal, and again, pay what they want.

Let's begin by doing our homework. Before we narrow it down to what you are going to buy, and where you are buying it, there are three very important things you need to know. How are you going to pay for it. Are you paying cash (as in real money, not borrowed), financing, or leasing.

If you are financing or leasing, what is your credit score.

What is your trade worth, if you have one.

Let's cover each of these before we move on.

Without a doubt, the most profitable department in every dealership is the finance department (or may be called the business office). Here, well trained salespeople do the paperwork for the purchase. They also encourage you to finance, buy extended service contracts (warranties), rustproofing, glass etching, and many other products. They will put anywhere from $1000 to $5000 of profit to the dealership on each car on average. This money is coming out of your pocket. The profit of this department is usually more than the rest of the dealership combined. Let's work through the three scenario's on how you intend to pay for the car. I realize you may not know at this point. I have heard "It depends" a million times, and "I don't know what I can afford" too. We will work through those as we go.

Cash: If you are in the fortunate position to pay cash for your vehicle, you will not be a welcome guest in the finance office. These salespeople not only get paid commission on what they produce in profit, but are also judged on their per car average profit. A cash deal not only makes them work for free, but may stop them from getting a bonus at the end of the month for a high per car profit average. They will try everything they can to get you to finance, and will talk about all kinds of reasons why your money is better off in the bank, and monthly payments make more sense. If that tactic doesn't work, they will really work hard to push extended warranties and other add ons. I'll talk about these warranties later, but if you are able to pay cash, stick to your guns and pay cash. Not only does the dealership make a profit on financing the vehicle for you, it is much easier to sell add on products. Psychologically, a buyer will feel it is easier to swallow a $20 or $30 a month increase in a payment over time for a warranty, than taking an additional $2000 out of their pocket.

Financing: There are basically two types of financing in a dealership. If they are a new car franchise, the manufacturer usually offers financing on their vehicles (new). You hear a lot about 0% or .9% but usually comes with a price. If you don't go with the low finance offer, there is generally a rebate (discount) that you could get as an alternative. Here's a typical example so you can see how it would work.

Let's say you are buying a car for $25,000. In this example, let's finance the entire amount. The manufacturer is offering a 0% for 60 months interest rate on this model, or a $3000 rebate if you don't take the financing offer. It's easy to figure out the payments at 0%. Just divide $25000 by the number of payments, which is $417 a month for 60 months, or 60 payments. If you went with the rebate instead, you would be paying $22,000 for the car. If you found a lender to give you the loan for 3% for 60 months, your payment would be $395 a month, or a savings of $22 a month, or $1,320 over the course of the loan term. At 4%, your payment would be $405 a month. To figure out your payment, there are all kinds of car loan calculators on the internet. And you should be able to find what offers the manufacturer is offering on their models also. Used cars don't typically offer low rates, unless it is a Certified used car. You would be wise to know what the payments are, and what you can afford by using one of these calculators before you venture in to buy a car. If you do take a rebate instead of an alternative low interest rate, you will pay less tax on the purchase price, and you will owe less on the loan, if for some reason you need to get out of the car, or it gets totaled in an accident.

Car loans are big business for banks. They make a fair profit by getting the money at a certain rate, then lending it out to you at a higher rate. It's that simple. Car dealerships do the same thing. They are financing the car with money that they get at a rate you qualify for (the buy rate) then write the financing contract at a higher rate, the difference is their profit. They are shopping around with multiple lenders to see what it would cost them for lending money to you. This is why it's important to know your credit score. The majority of credit scores fall in the high 400 to low 800 range. The higher the score, the better rate you will get. This is because a low score indicates that you may have trouble making, or wanting to pay, your payments. And the last thing a lender wants to do is chase you around for money every month, or repossess the car. That costs the lender money. A score of 700, called Tier 1, or higher will always get you the best rates. All states have limits on the rates they can charge high risk customers, and can go as high as 23%. As you have seen, the rate you get will affect the payment, sometimes dramatically. Just in the example above, a 1% increase on that particular loan increased the payment $9 a month. But that's $540 over the course of that loan, and that's a very common example. The finance department will usually mark up the loan they are doing for you by anywhere from one to 3 percent. This is called the finance reserve. You can negotiate this. The finance person would rather give you the loan at cost than have you pay cash. It helps their loan penetration average, and may help them sell add on products at a monthly cost instead of trying to get you to pay for them all at once. Make sure you negotiate the interest rate before you talk other items. If they think you are not going to buy anything else, they may not budge on the rate. At the very least, you should shop around for a rate at the bank you use, or credit union, or even your insurance company. You can do a lot of this over the phone or internet. Knowing this information beforehand will give you the edge on negotiating the rate. Just make sure you get their best rate you can before you show your cards. Otherwise, they may just match your deal if they know what it is, and could have given you a better deal if you kept that information to yourself.

Unfortunately, people with poor credit, no matter what the reason, always end up paying more for financing. It's just a risk management cost. It also keeps those people on that never ending cycle of just trying to keep up, since everything costs more. One of the most important things you can do for yourself, is to build and maintain your credit. I understand that all kinds of things can ruin it, medical bills, divorce, loss of work, etc. There are really three parts to a credit report. The first part has your personal information, jobs and addresses going back a few years, and any judgements or liens against you, both current and past, paid or not. The second section has what they call your short term revolving accounts. These are credit cards, personal loans, and any other unsecured loans (no collateral). They show your current balance, length of time you have had the loan, monthly payment, and your payment history over the course of the loan. The last section is your house, cars, and student loans. Again it will show current balance, payment amount, and history. The credit score is a formula that rates you on how you pay your bills, and your ability to repay the loan back, based on how much money you owe, how much monthly obligation you have, and an estimate of your income. Car loans and house loans have different criteria they use, so the scores will vary by what you are trying to buy. It has been studied and proven that most people will pay their auto loans before almost any other bill. They need their cars to get to work in able to make money to pay all those other bills. This has not gone unnoticed by the lenders, and even if you have questionable credit in your loans, if you make your car payments on time, they are more likely to lend you the money. Of course, everyone knows you can get your score for free on the internet. It is in your best interest to know this before you go shopping for a loan.

One last thing about credit. Even knowing your score, 90% of consumers still are apprehensive about their ability to purchase and get financed. I have great credit, but I still get butterflies in my stomach when applying for a loan.

Dealerships know this and use it to their advantage. When they come back and joyously proclaim "you're approved" they know you have a certain amount of relief, and are then more susceptible to just take what terms they give you. The other thing they know, is that a person who knows they have great credit or paying cash comes from a position of strength, and most likely harder to deal with. The typical salesperson and finance person would always rather deal with someone with a bit spotty credit, so they have more control, and control is what negotiating for a car is all about.

Leasing: Leasing is like renting. It is simply a contract between you and the manufacturer of the car for a specified amount of time and a specified amount of miles. You are required to provide insurance and license plates on the vehicle, keep up with any scheduled maintenance intervals required (like oil changes, tire rotation, etc.), and return the car in proper mechanical and physical condition. Which means it has to run, not be all beat up, and doesn't need tires or brakes. They do allow a certain amount of wear and tear for scratches and dings, and if you are hard on a car, there are wear and tear warranties that will cover more damage for a fee.

Why is leasing good for the manufacturer? Because the payment for the consumer is lower than purchasing, it helps them to sell more cars. The reason the payment is lower is that you are only paying for a portion of the car, the time and miles you use, instead of the entire car. There are 3 things which determine what the payment will be on any particular model of car. One of course is the selling price, then the residual value, which is what the predicted value of the car will be when the lease is over, given the miles and age of the car, and the interest rate. Residuals (or future values) are merely guesses, because there are unforeseen events that can change the value of the used car over time. Recalls, emission scandals, repair history, and consumer ratings just to name a few. The manufacturer relies on an independent firm to determine the future value. As an example, the car you are looking to purchase may be worth half of its value in three years with 45,000 miles on it. They would set the residual at 50%. You would be paying on the 50% you use. If you change the predicted miles and term of the car, you will change the residual and thus the payment. The higher the residual, the lower the payment and vice versa. The third thing that determines the payment is called the money factor. It is simply the interest rate, which is expressed as a decimal. If you multiply the money factor by 2400, it will give you a fairly accurate estimate of the interest rate. Example: Money factor is .0014. .0014 X 2400 = 3.36%. Of course the dealership marks up the rate on the lease when they are able to. They can't change the residual however. That is set on the contract, and only a change in more, or less miles or different length of the lease will change that.

Not only do leases help sell more cars, it also lets the manufacturer predict when someone will need a new one, so they can match production, because generally most people return their lease instead of buying the car at the end, and get a new one. It also keeps people tied to the dealership for service, which promotes a better experience for the customer for that vehicle, since everything is usually covered under the manufacturer warranty, and they will hopefully be a repeat customer, and buy another of the same make. It also provides a reliable source of used inventory for the used car department, and lease returns are some of the better used cars to be able to sell. They are one owner, well maintained, and locally owned. The manufacturer realizes that a lot of first time car buyers buy used, and hope the good experience they have with their used car will bring them back to buy a new one when they can afford to do so. Negotiating the price of the car is one thing, and we will get into that, but finding out the money factor is a bit trickier. They are not easy to find, and I have found the best way to find out, is when you are shopping around for a vehicle by phone or the internet, just ask what the buy rate is. The buy rate is the unmarked up money factor. Most salesman will be so eager to get you in to buy, they will spill the beans and drop down to the buy rate. The finance department blows up when this happens.

So why should you consider leasing? Let's face it, people like cars, and for many reasons want a new one. The average consumer gets a different car, new or used, about every 3 to 4 years. That just happens to coincide (not by coincidence) with the term of most leases, and it used to be the average retail loan length, before cars got so expensive that everyone had to lengthen the term of the loan, to be able to afford one. So if you like to get a new car every 3 years, then leasing provides a way to avoid the hassle of selling or trading your old one. The payments are usually less than financing, and cars are not an investment, they are an expense. They go down in value every month, so whether you pay cash, finance or lease, a car costs you money. The less per month the better. If you intend to keep your car for a long time, which a lot of people say but then never do, leasing may still make sense if the incentives to lease are so enticing, you can purchase the car at the end of the lease for the residual value, and it's yours. Here is an example of how that may work for you.

Let's buy that same car for $25000, and finance it for the lowest payment we found, $395 a month for 60 months. After 5 years, you have shelled out $23700, remember it had the $3000 rebate to bring the price down to $22,000. A typical lease will run about $100 a month less. So if we leased that same car, and let's say the residual, or buy out at the end, is 50%, you can buy the car for $12500. The residual is always calculated off the MSRP, not the selling price, which is of great advantage to the consumer. In this case, your 36 payments on the lease will be $10620. You are going to buy the car for $12500. Total cost is $23120. You are only saving $580, but I wanted to show you a close example to focus on some other benefits you might overlook. If you have ever heard of the term, upside down, it means that you owe more on the car than it's worth. You can cure that by putting a lot of money down, but that doesn't change the fact that cars depreciate, much faster in the beginning of their lifecycle, then at the end. Because a lease has a guaranteed price you can purchase the car for at the end of the lease contract, you are in control of any unforeseen events that may change its value. One may be that they become extremely popular, and you can purchase the car for less than it's worth, keep it or sell it, and you have come out well. On the other hand, if they are a complete dud of a car, and the value drops to nothing, you can walk away when the contract is over and owe nothing. So in essence, nothing to lose, but everything to gain. And if you do like to get a newer model for safety, style or whatever reason every 3 years or so, you avoid the hassle of trading or selling your car on your own. Even being in the business, I would never sell my own car from my house. Too many strange people and things turn up, and I look at it like a safety risk. Also, if something happens the day after they buy the car from me, I'm not taking it back, or fixing it, even though I would certainly feel bad. Lastly, you will always have a car under warranty if you do get a new car every 3 years. That in itself can save you a lot of money should something happen. So whether you lease, finance or pay cash is a personal and financial decision for you, and you alone. It's good to understand how it all works so you can have options and choose the best path for you.

After all that, you are probably thinking you need a break. And you are probably also thinking it still depends on how I buy my car when I find one. That's ok. A good salesperson will show you all of your options for buying, that information was just for you to be aware of how it all works. While we are talking about that terrific salesperson, the majority of salespeople don't have a full grasp of leasing and financing. They are just getting the information from the manager. I'll get into that later, but no matter what, and I will mention this several times, don't be in a panic to buy the day you walk in. No deal is ever too good to be true, and there will always be another car. If you don't know for certain how you want to buy the car, then get the information, go home to give you time to analyze it, then go back.

The financing scenarios we covered dealt mostly with new vehicles, so let's finish up with new and dealing on price. I will get into the very important trade value in a bit. I will assume that at this point you have selected the make and model you are interested in buying. At least down to two or three. The next step is to get the best price, which always requires getting a price from more than one dealership. In today's information world, you can get as many prices as you want in minutes, but huge numbers are not necessary. Probably just confuse you more and make the whole process unmanageable. First you need to decide how far you would travel to get your vehicle, because buying from your closest dealer always makes the most sense. Let's say you decide you would only drive 100 miles, more than that would be too much effort, then look up those dealers who carry your desired brand, and contact the dealership either by phone or internet. Internet is preferred, because then you have everything in writing, you have time to do your homework, and you won't be swayed by a salesperson who is very persuasive on the phone. The number one goal of the dealership when dealing with phone calls, is to give as little info as possible and get the customer to come in. That way they can a lot more control.

Please don't pay for buying a car from a broker. You won't, I repeat, won't get a better price than doing it on your own. In fact, most dealers don't want to work with brokers, and blow them off. Go ahead and use big box buying services if you like, it's a place to start to get a price, and you can work from there. The only exception is if you have way more money than time. A broker will work the deal for you, and deliver the car right to your work or home. It's a service that comes with a price.

CHAPTER 3
THE TRADE

When you are getting pricing, be honest, be nice, and understand you are working with a real person just trying to do their job on the other end. Your goal here is to get a fair price, not something for nothing. Once you have collected your offers, then is the time to contact your preferred dealership to buy from, and make an appointment to come in and test drive. Do not, I repeat, do not reveal your competing bids, at this time. Now you may even want to pay more for not having the hassle of driving out of town for a car. I have had clients pay as much as a thousand dollars more to buy from me. Good service is worth something, you should decide how much it is worth to you.

Now you have gotten some competing prices, checked your credit score, are aware of how the financing works, and ready to enter a dealership to test drive and select your vehicle. In getting the pricing, you most likely have a contact at the dealership already too. Try to go in when they are there, because salespeople hate it when someone comes in asking for a specific person, and they aren't there, and they have to end up helping you. It's called a split, and you will end up getting usually poor service, and may end up getting in the middle of a pissing match, yes, it can be that childish. All in all, you should be prepared for a really good experience, as dealerships understand the value of a customer for life, and they will bend over backwards to make you one. Oh, just one more thing, as Columbo would say, I have a trade.

Never, never, ever, ever bring up the fact that you intend to trade your existing car before getting a rock solid final price on what you are buying. Tell them you have it sold, it got totaled, you are getting an extra car, anything, but leave the trade out of the deal. They aren't going to believe you anyway, because almost 80% of consumers will trade their car. Let's face it, selling a car on your own is tough. Lots of downsides to doing that even though you may save a few bucks. It is better to trade for many reasons, and if your state gives a tax break for doing so, which most do, the difference between selling it on your own and trading may not be that great. Dealerships want trades, it's a huge profit center for them. A car on the lot with a story, especially a trade versus something bought at the auction without know it's history, will always sell faster and command a higher price. That being said, they want to take them in for as little cost as they can, and who can blame them. So when you are all done with your price negotiations, then bring up the fact that you would like to trade your car. You are about to discover what it's actually worth.

I have appraised literally thousands of vehicles in my 28 year career. I am really good at it, and would consider myself an expert. You know what the real value of your car is worth? I don't know and neither does anyone else. It's what the next person will pay for it. We might make an extremely educated guess, but in the end, time will be the determining factor if you guessed right or wrong. A trade appraisal varies from individual to individual, region to region, but they are all pretty much the same. First you have to drive the car to figure out if it needs any mechanical repairs, and inspect for physical damage. Tires, brakes, dents, dings, scratches, glass repair, things not working, etc. After that, it's mostly computer work. First you check the vehicle history, like a Carfax report, and try to find any maintenance history either from records in the glove box, or if it was purchased from you, then your service department.

Then you have to see if there are any upcoming scheduled maintenances due, like timing belts, that can be very expensive. All these things have dollar values, and either have to be remedied before selling, or maybe not, but the asking price will be reduced. If it has been in an accident, that will also affect the value. Now I have determined how much it will cost me to put the car on the lot for sale, or if too much needs to be done, may just wholesale the car to a dealer, or send it to the auction.

The next step is to find out what the market says. I try to find out a retail value first, what similar vehicles are selling for in the area, and if I can, how long it has been taking to sell them at that price. They are my competitors, so I know in order to sell mine, I will probably have to enter the market slightly lower. At this point, I know what my top sale price is, I now deduct the money I will spend to get it ready to sell, and then build in a profit. I now have an idea of what I can pay the customer for it. Now I have to justify that price. I do that by looking at a few different sources. A good one in our area is KBB, which gives you trade, private party, and retail values. If a dealer is using KBB to justify a value, they will always start with

Trade In Value Fair Condition. Be aware of that when you are doing your own research. Edmunds is used but not so much where I worked. NADA and Black Book are also popular. Most people are aware of these sites, and will know what they have said about their trade before they come in, and so should you. I also look at what is available to buy, and what has recently sold at the auction. If I can go out and replace the same or similar vehicle at the auction, then I have a better idea of what I should pay. Many time I will pick up the phone and call a wholesaler for a bid if I don't want the car for my lot. If it's a make I am not franchised for, I may call an appraiser at a store that is, because they generally can get more for a car they sell new. After I have determined its ACV (actual cash value), built in a profit for the store, and able to find an online value that justifies my appraisal, I am ready to present it to the customer. A good salesperson may serve the numbers, or a manager or appraiser might. Obviously, the dealership wants to take the vehicle in for a little as they can, so many times will send the salesperson in first, serve up low numbers to start with in case they get lucky and the customer takes it, or the manager can come in later, give them a little more, and save the day.

As an example of never knowing, here's what happened to one of my salespeople. One day I was listening to him on the phone arguing with a customer about a trade. "Look, you told me you didn't have a trade when I gave you my numbers. If you bring that trade over here, we are going to steal it. I mean it. Bring it here, and we will steal it". We had a good chuckle about it when he hung up, even though I could tell he was mad about it. Then guess what. About two hours later they showed up with their trade, and we stole it. He was still mad about it and gave them at least 2 thousand dollars less than what it was worth, I know because I sold it a week later and made $6500 gross. You just never know.

Here's the reason I don't want you to bring up the trade before you make your best pricing deal. Dealerships know that customers are sensitive to the value of their current cars. A lot of people have emotional attachments, don't really see all that is wrong with their cars, feel the repairs don't really cost that much, and have unrealistic expectations as to their value. And they think they should get retail. Doesn't work that way. So if a dealership knows you are trading, they will hold some profit in the sale of their car, to over allow money on yours. The value of the trade is the same to them, but by giving you more, makes you feel better. You see it happen more often on used cars at some dealerships. They have their cars priced very high, more than they are worth, and give the customers big trade values. The customers focus only on the trade amount, and end up paying too much anyway.

You can focus on trade values, price for the new one, whatever you want, but in the end, the only way to truly compare offers from different dealerships is the difference in the amount you pay between yours and theirs, and the payment amount. It's that simple.

I have to admit, I have never had a customer tell me that I was giving them too much for their trade. Well I did once, but that's rare. Almost everyone will say the opposite, it's not enough. So knowing that, the dealership will always pay more, how much depends on how bad they want to sell a car, but they will always move. Don't be afraid to ask for more. No one is going to mad at you, and they aren't going to kick you out. You aren't going to get retail, what you want is to be treated fairly. The dealership has a right to a profit once again, and they are taking all the risks that they can successfully retail your trade for a profit, and that they assume any risk that something major may happen, like a motor or transmission failure, that may cost them thousands. Once again, do your homework on your trade before you get to the dealership. Go online to see what they are retailing for, leave out private party prices because most of those people are unrealistic, and look up trade values on the major car sites.

Here is a very important point that you need to remember. Never get so emotionally wrapped up in buying a car that you are afraid to walk out without buying. Or that you have put in so much time doing this, you just want to get it over with. In fact, you should never buy on your first visit anyway. I know the dealership will tell you all kinds of things to get you to buy right then, because they know statistically that once you leave, you have a good chance of never coming back. Only good for today, one of a kind, aren't going to get this deal tomorrow, you name it. Even the most savvy buyer will get caught up in the heat of the moment. Walk away, and reason it all out with a cool head. Once you come back, you will feel better that you are making a good decision, and you probably are.

I used to use this close when I was selling cars and it was extremely effective. I would take the sale as far as I could, then the manager would come in and try to close them. He was a pretty intense guy, and would close lots of deals. The ones he didn't, I would just follow them out to their car, where they felt comfortable, jump in the back seat as they sat in the front, and would simply ask why they didn't say yes. I had built up a certain amount of trust with them, so they usually would be very honest, now that the pressure and stress was off, and tell me what their objections were. We would just talk and work it out right there in the car, and more often than not, would come right back in and finish up the purchase. In fact, and it's very true, that you will never know that you have gotten the best possible deal until you get up and walk out. These people became my best repeat customers and sent me the most referrals. The ones my manager closed I usually never saw or heard from them again.

It's no secret that people come to dealerships to buy cars, and the dealership is there to sell them. As much as people beat around the bush on both sides, it comes down to that. Try to make it as enjoyable as possible. Now let's talk about buying a used car. A lot of the process is the same, but if you intend to buy used, here are some of the things to watch for

CHAPTER 4
BUYING A USED CAR

The market for used cars is huge. It's larger than the new car market. There are many good reasons to buy a used vehicle. Certainly, depreciation from new is one of them. Which makes them less money to buy. Sometimes, a model has been replaced, and you like the old one better. Insurance rates are less. You can get more features in a used than a new one for the same payment, and on and on.

There are also more places to purchase one. Private party, small used car lots, rental agencies, used car superstores like Carmax, and of course, franchised dealers. I have nothing against small used car lots, in fact I have many friends in that business, but try to buy your used car from a new car franchised dealer or a national chain used car dealership. They are firmly rooted in the community, care deeply about customer satisfaction, and have the financial clout in case something goes wrong. Many have great return policies and back their cars up with warranties. And try not to buy your car from a private party, unless you personally know them, and even then, it's caveat emptor (buyer beware). Chances are you can't return it, and if it breaks a mile down the road, you are on your own. Here are a few different sources where used cars come from on dealer lots.

Trade ins: We have been talking about yours, so that is one source. Trade ins are cars that people who own them trade in, or are cars that the leases are up, and people turn them into the dealership and get something else. Typically, a dealership likes trade ins as there are no fees to get to them (auction fees, transportation). If the vehicle was purchased from them originally, hopefully there will be a good maintenance history that is easy to access. And the fact that they returned to you to buy another car, they either liked the car or the dealership or both. That makes a good story to help sell it. Trades typically also sell faster than other sources of vehicles. You may want to look for trades at dealerships that carry the same brand in new cars. As mentioned, someone that had good luck with their car, will buy another of the same make, and that is a good sign.

Street buys: These are cars that a lot of dealers advertise for. We Buy Your Car is in a lot of ads, and also signage around the property. Similar to trades, they are trying to save fees, and have a good local story to tell. The value they place on these cars is the same as trades (ACV), and they generally pay the salesperson a flat commission to get one. That drives salespeople to search for them, either in the paper, online, or parked in someone's yard.

If these cars have a maintenance history available, and a good accident history, they are excellent used cars for you to purchase. However, I have known many people who don't take care of their cars. They don't change oil when due (one person I knew drove their truck 120,000 miles before he changed oil), they smoke in them, ignore transmission and brake flushes, and beat them. You can't always tell, because the dealership does a great job of reconditioning and the car looks brand new. And that is the number 1 reason why someone is attracted and buy one used car over another, the look of it. So if you are shopping for a used vehicle, take utmost care that you try to find one that was cared for, and if it has been, you may be able to contact the previous owner to verify. They will be glad to do so because they feel proud to have taken care of it. Someone who beat and neglected their car will not want to talk to you.

Rental agencies: Rental cars are the ones that get rented at the airport, when people crash their cars, or whenever someone needs to rent a car. Millions of them are purchased by the rental car companies each year, put into use for a period of time, then sold either at auction, or directly to dealerships. It's a great source of cars for a dealership, because there are plenty of them around and will generally get delivered to you free of charge. Unfortunately, because every dealership has access and buys them, the profit margins are extremely small, and you are competing with everyone else for the sale. The information that they were a rental car will show up on the history report. Here's the good and bad for the consumer. The good: Rental agencies will maintain their vehicles, post no smoking signs in them, and get rid of them still under the manufacturer warranty. The bad: Each vehicle could have literally hundreds of drivers, and you can imagine how some people drive. Usually the rental company is trying to save money, so the better options are generally not in these cars. They always sell for thousands less than new, because the rental company has taken in income from them. I for one think they are a good value.

Other dealers: Used car departments are under a lot of pressure to quickly move their inventory off the lot. Seasonal variations in demand, year of vehicle, lot rot (when a vehicle deteriorates just sitting there) and monthly values dropping are just some of the things that affect the value. Dealership groups will generally have a system in place to trade cars amongst themselves before the car gets more than 90 days on the lot. After 90 days, they generally are a loss to sell one. Just that fact they move to a different location, with different buyers driving through, the care may sell in a day somewhere else. You always have to be a bit skeptical about cars that have been sitting on a dealer's lot for too long. It may be a low demand vehicle, which will ultimately affect you when it comes time to trade again, or there may be something wrong with it. There is no way for the consumer to find out how long it has been on the lot, short of asking the salesperson, and hope they are honest.

Auction: There are two types of auctions, open and closed. A closed sale at an auction house is one that is only available for franchised dealers of that particular make (Like Ford, Dodge, BMW, Chevrolet). These are cars that are usually lease returns that the dealer turned down, or turned in at a dealer who did not originate the lease in the first place. There are also company cars driven by corporate employees. There are also buy backs. Buy backs are vehicles that have been bought back by the manufacturer from the original customer under a lemon law or similar. That will also show up on the history report and will have documentation that you will have to sign showing that you were aware of the issue. Some states, like California, have very strict buy back laws, and cars may be returned for just about anything. I have seen everything from engine failures to someone allergic to the air conditioning.

The second type of sale is the open sale, where anyone with a dealer license can bid and buy. These cars can and do end up with dealers with 1000 cars on the lot, to dealers with 2 cars on the lot, or maybe someone just buys it for themselves. Whichever type of sale, closed or open, doesn't necessarily mean that the vehicle is physically at the auction. Many of these cars are still at the dealerships where they are turned in or on the lot for sale. Once sold, then a truck comes and picks them up. The price the car finally sells for after either being bid at the auction itself or online, is the highest that anyone looking is willing to pay. In a sense, this is the most accurate way of valuing any vehicle, as it is the real exchange of dollars. What is something worth is what someone will pay for it.

Shopping for a used car is a little different than new, because each car is slightly different which makes negotiating on one different too. Dealerships count on this when selling them, and it is these cars that make them the most money. There is no hard and fast rule, but the majority of dealers will price a fresh trade on the lot with a two to six thousand dollar gross (the selling price minus the cost). There is no possible way for you to know their cost of a used vehicle, not even if you traded it in. In the cost of the vehicle, real money they had to shell out, is the price they paid or gave the customer for it, reconditioning, shop repairs, paint work, glass repair, you get the picture. The gross they make on a car is not all profit. There are many costs to a dealership, and it's frightening how little profit goes to the bottom line. That does not concern you or your negotiation. A manager will only look at the fixed gross (selling price minus real cost) to determine whether or not to sell the car. Some dealerships let their salespeople know the cost of the cars, some don't. Many cars are sold at a loss. Here are some of the reasons.

Bid the car wrong.

Needed too many repairs.

Wrong time of year.

Wrong color or model.

On the lot too long.

Bad history report.

Need one more deal to hit bonus.

The car you are trading yours in on needs to go away.

Customer was a good negotiator.

That's the one you are going to be, the customer was a good negotiator.

One thing you should always do when buying a used car is have a skilled mechanic inspect the vehicle, not one at the dealership obviously, if the vehicle is out of manufacturer warranty, or if you feel there may be something amiss. The dealership should provide you with an inspection report. Get a copy right away, and question any items on it that may not have been resolved. Any needed repairs not done will cost you money to remedy, and you need to get these resolved before you buy the car. Afterward, you are on your own.

The other thing to get and keep is a copy of the history report, a common one being CarFax. The dealer should gladly provide one free of charge, and if they don't, that's a red flag. You can easily get one yourself off the internet. All you need is the VIN (vehicle identification number) to get one. Here is what you should look for.

Vin number: Make sure that the vehicle identification number on the Carfax matches the car. If not, you have a report on a different vehicle.

Mileage: The left hand column will have mileage milestones. When the car was originally purchased, changes of ownership, accidents, buy back info, and many other events. It's important that the end mileage reflects what is currently on the car, and that there is no break in the mileage history, a common one being the miles don't follow a sequential order. This is a red flag and should stop the sale until further investigation.

Ownership: The right hand column will give a history of who owned the car. Personal use, rental agency, company car, lease, you name it. If what the salesperson said about ownership is different on the Carfax, another red flag. This column will sometimes show maintenance history, if available.

Warranty: The report will tell you when the warranty started, the type of warranty, and if you have any left.

Here's the Caveat. Any history report will only show the traceable things that are reported. Everyone knows that an accident devalues your vehicle. Some people will pay cash to get their car fixed to avoid this showing up. Flood cars are especially troubling. A vehicle may be purchased at an auction, and sold to the end user, before the history is even reported, and it's no one's fault. Never, ever buy a vehicle with a salvage title, no matter how good a deal it seems.

There is nothing wrong with buying a used vehicle over a new one. In fact, there are many people who will never buy new. You just have to be a bit more diligent and research the vehicle.

CHAPTER 5
ONE PRICE OR NEGOTIATING
DEALER

Let's go back and revisit the one price, no haggle type of dealership. These dealerships price their cars, new and used, and advertise not to negotiate off that price. It's true and it's not.

True: One price dealerships have been around for a long time. There were some experimenting with the idea 30 years ago. A one price dealer, new and used, will research and price their inventory at what they say is a non-negotiating price. You pay, everyone pays. They do advertise this way, that is true.

False: They don't change the price. They do and will change the price. Depending on incentive changes on new, and value changes in used, such as age, they adjust prices, maybe daily, weekly, or monthly, whatever the case may be. They will also adjust to price match.

True: The salespeople are trained to stick with the pricing. They are not allowed to alter or change the price of a vehicle. Only the manager can do that.

False: They won't reduce the price. If a customer presents a lower price from another dealer, they will change the price to match the deal. If you make an offer lower than what they are asking, they may say it's due for a price adjustment anyway, so will change the price. Or they may give you something else to sweeten the deal, like throw in floor mats, bed liner, or maybe even a warranty.

True: Many dealerships will advertise that their salespeople are not paid commission. This is meant to give you the impression that there is no financial benefit for the salesperson to hard sell you a car.

False: There are many ways that salespeople get paid, but it is not an hourly wage. There is always a financial incentive, whether it paid on gross, volume, customer satisfaction, or a combination of all three. One price stores will usually pay a draw, then bonuses based on the volume of cars you sell. They need to sell cars to make money, and to keep their job.

True: They sometimes let you walk (leave the dealership) with a price in hand. We call it a shopping ticket, meaning you now have a tool to get another dealer to give you a matching or better deal.

False: This is their best deal, not. If you truly are in the market for a car, and not just tire kicking while your spouse is at the mall, a dealer will call you back and offer you an incentive to come back in. This is how you get a deal. If they don't, you probably have a pretty good deal, and now you have your shopping ticket.

A negotiating dealership is just that, they will negotiate everything. They always have gross built into their prices to allow for that. If a dealership is not advertising that they are a one price store, then you know that you need to negotiate the price, your trade, the financing, everything. They expect that. In fact, if you don't, they will assume that you aren't really serious, or have so many credit issues you can't buy.

CHAPTER 6
STEPS TO THE SALE

Salespeople go through training when they get hired. The process they go through is probably not unlike a lot of other retail training for big ticket items, It's called STEPS TO THE SALE. There are numerous variations on this theme, but here is the basic training.

Meet and Greet: This is where the salesperson greets you and starts the process of building rapport and gaining control. Big smile, handshake, welcome to... It is said that the sale is made or lost in the first 30 seconds. This may or not be true, but if the salesperson makes an initial bad impression, it will be a lot tougher for them to sell you a car, just human behavior. 90% of getting hired as a salesperson is the way can build trust, confidence, and put someone at ease. Let's face it, some people are better at it than others. A professional look and pleasing personality is definitely half the battle. They will give you a business card, and try to get your name and contact number, just in case you slip away, they can follow you up. They also need it in case the manager spots them talking to you, they will get their you know what chewed for not getting it.

Qualify: Once the salesperson has introduced themselves, they are ready to see if you are indeed in the market, and can afford to buy one. This is also the step where they see how much control they are starting to have with you. If you follow them around like a puppy, then they have. It is also the step to try to land (or pick a car out) that they can start to sell. This step may take a few minutes, if you have done your research, know what you want to buy, and they have it right there in stock. This is also called the **Investigation Step,** because now is when they start asking you everything they learned to ask in training. They will try to find your Hot Buttons, things that mean the most to you, and tailor their presentation around those things.

Walk Around: This is the product presentation, once they think you have some interest in a particular vehicle. It starts by a calculated outside demo, designed to hit your hot buttons (the things that may interest you the most, like horsepower, safety, style). It is the first step to start getting you emotionally involved with the vehicle. An emotionally involved customer is one that is always easier to close. If they do their job correctly, and have found a vehicle you are interested in, and can afford to buy, they will end the demo by having you sit either behind the wheel, or in the passenger seat, which gets them ready for the next step. A good salesperson will get you to go, even if you don't want to. At this stage, they will ask for your license and insurance card, just in case. The information gets loaded into the dealership CRM (Customer Relations Management), a program which will be used from everything to writing up the deal, sending you birthday cards, triggering follow up milestones, and putting any personal information that you may share with them.

Test Drive: Obviously, you want to drive a car before you buy it. So this is where the rubber hits the road (that's good). This is really where the buying choice gets narrowed down, either you like it or you don't. If you do, you move on, if you don't, it goes back a step to pick out another car. It is also where the salesperson gets to build that rapport and get you more emotionally involved. They know there is some apprehension at the dealership, happens to everyone, and getting away from there, out on a predetermined test route, winding roads and all, takes a bit of the pressure off. Now they can talk about the car, you, themselves, and get you to feel more committed because they are taking all this time and effort to help you. When you arrive back at the dealership, and have expressed interest in the vehicle, they will have you pull it up to the door, because other people are also looking at this car, and they want to make sure you have first dibbs. It is also what they call a trail close. If you just want to park it back in the space it came from, they think they have the wrong vehicle. If you pull it up into the sold area, then you have made a gesture that you want to buy it.

Write Up: Now is the time they pop the big question. Do you want to buy the car? There a thousand ways to ask for the sale, and during the entire presentation so far, they have been guiding you down the path to the sale by asking mini closing questions. And you have probably been unaware this has been happening. One of my favorites at this point is, after they sit you down in their office with free coffee in hand, will say "Did you want to put this in your name, or both names?" Boom. Either answer lets them know you are buying it. Obviously, you have been asking all kinds of questions, getting them answered, and if you are hesitant at this stage, they will either go back to select a different car they can close you on, or get a manager involved (another face) to see what may be the issue.

Let's assume you are at the stage of buying, and allow the salesperson to get numbers on what they will sell it to you for, your trade, and payments. All this information will come from the manager, and if the salesperson has done their job well, built trust in themselves and showed value in the vehicle, they will get the numbers, present them to you, and wrap it up. By now I hope you realize that this is just the start.

Close: Here is a funny thing about salespeople, some love to close the deal, and others live in fear to get this far. It is by far the most talked about and trained on part of the sale. This is where they either get paid or they don't. If a salesperson has done their job well, and you feel committed and emotionally attached to the car, then the close may take but a few minutes. And it takes time and patience to do all of the above steps to build value. Other salespeople, especially the more experienced ones, do the Meet and Greet, then go right to the close. They don't want to waste a lot of time and effort, and will skip a lot of steps to do just that. You will get both kinds if you shop several places. I'm going to move on to the final step, because the close is where the negotiations all come in, and I will cover that separately.

The Delivery: Everyone is happy now. The pressure is off. You agreed to the terms, signed all the paperwork, and ready to drive away. You may just get the keys tossed to you, and hear "hit the bricks", but I doubt it. Every salesperson has a vested interest in starting you out with your new vehicle in a positive way. And they also want you to come back for your service needs. So a good salesperson will show you all the features, take your picture for the dealership Facebook page, give you a tour of the facility, introduce you to the managers you may not have met, show you where to drive in for service, etc.... You may even be coached a bit about getting a survey from them and the manufacturer, and their livelihood depends on a perfect score. In a way this is true. Dealerships have a financial incentive to get good scores, and a salesperson is not going to stay employed there if they have a record of low CSI (Customer Satisfaction Index) scores. Some even get paid on perfect surveys. The salesperson also knows that if you are happy, you won't get buyer's remorse and want to return the car the next day, and if you are happy, will return in the future and refer your friends to them. None of this is bad, and you will want to learn everything there is to know about your car. Take time, ask questions. If you use what is in this book, you will have a good experience and have chosen a vehicle, gotten the deal you want, and have no remorse.

That is basically the process you will encounter at the dealership. Like I said, every salesperson is different, they all have their own way of dealing with people, but the process will be similar. Now that you know what's going on, you might get some amusement keeping track of the steps as you go along. The salesperson might even get a chuckle too if you let him know what you know.

And you shouldn't try to rush through it either. You may learn that the vehicle you were so sure you wanted, is not the right one for you after all. Let them do their job, they are the ones that know the product (I hope they do), and will steer you away from cars that are maybe questionable, and show you things you may have missed. After all, they do want what is best for you. You will not be a repeat customer for them if you don't even like the car you get.

CHAPTER 7
NEGOTIATING

This is the fun part. For the dealer that is. Maybe for you too if that's what you like to do. This is the number one thing that salespeople are trained on. This is what they talk about every day. They read, watch training videos, role play and get coached by managers on every deal. This is their living.

THIS IS IMPORTANT: Salespeople are trained that if they do their job right on the lot, the close will only take a few minutes. That is true. **IF YOU DO YOUR JOB BEFORE YOU GO TO THE DEALERSHIP THE CLOSE WILL ONLY TAKE A FEW MINUTES**. Take your time in a non-emotional and non-stress environment to do your homework. Reading and understanding what is here in this book is part of your homework.

A dealership may have anywhere from a couple of salespeople, to over a hundred. And they all have different talents and skill levels. The ideal situation is when the salesperson takes the customer through the whole process, and closes the deal themselves. These always have the highest gross and the happiest customers. Some dealerships have Closers whose only role is to go in and close the customer. The manager is mostly used as a last resort on terms, or when the sale gets bogged down, and the salesperson loses control, and is in danger of the customer leaving. Managers can always tell when a salesperson has done their job or not, so a lot of times the salesperson will try to dismiss the customer if they haven't done a good job and get them out the door before the manager finds out. Let's assume you got to the stage where you found a vehicle and are working on terms. We will start as the deal is presented.

It's called the first pencil. This is where the dealership will give you the numbers they will sell the car for, what your trade is worth, and lease or finance payments if you are not paying cash. It may be on a formal computer printout, on a worksheet, pad of paper, or a cocktail napkin (kidding). Doesn't matter, it's the numbers. If the salesperson has done their job well, one day only, deal of a lifetime, I can't believe you are getting this deal, then you may say yes, and buy it. The manager really doesn't expect this to happen. These are some of the things you may hear at this point.

The price: This is a fantastic price you are getting. I can't believe they will let it go for that. We take great pride on researching the market, and selling our cars for less than everyone else. That's a lot of car for this little money. I'm sure you can't get this deal anywhere else. Better take it or they may change their mind. I know other people are looking at this car, and it may be gone if you wait. You are absolutely stealing this car. I could go on and on but I think you get the picture.

The trade: That is an unbelievably good number on your car. I really told the manager to step up on your car, it's really nice. We took one in just like yours a few days ago, and they put nowhere near that kind of money in it. I think he messed up and is giving you too much. I have a buyer for your car, so we are paying more than it's worth because we have a quick sale coming. He didn't notice what was wrong with your car, let's take advantage of that. I really don't want to let you drive back home in yours today, it's not safe.

The payments: Good new, I didn't think the payments would be this low. That's only a few dollars more a month than you thought you would have to pay. Interest rates are going up, not sure if you can get this payment tomorrow. I know it's a bit higher than what you wanted to pay each month, but if we put a bit more down, or stretched out the terms, I am sure I could get you a lower payment.

Everything in a dealership is get you to say yes, and take delivery, today. They know if you leave, there is a very slim chance you will be back. Too much competition out there. Just look at all the ads on TV, it's all car ads (Beer, drugs, and makeup too). You need to use this to your advantage. I have said this before, never buy a car on your first visit, and I mean it. You will always get the same deal, and 90% of the time a better deal, by leaving. There is too much at stake for a dealership to risk losing a sale. Any dealership worth doing business with will always follow up and work for the business. If they don't, do you really think they will follow up with you if you do buy a car and have an issue with it later. The biggest reason to leave for you is that you now have time to let the ether (emotion) to subside, and you can study the deal more rationally. Let me give you an example.

It was 1989, and I had been selling cars for about a year. My Dad, who just retired, wanted to buy an Isuzu Trooper, a new one. My dealership didn't carry that brand, so I told my Dad I would help him buy one. There was an Isuzu dealer about a mile from his home, so we drove over there on my day off. Small dealer, 3 salespeople, 20 cars on the lot. We met one, he took us out for a demo, got all of our information, gave us the figures, and asked for the sale. I didn't tell him I sold cars too. Before we went, I told my Dad not to buy that day, even though he wanted to, so we gave the old "I want to think about it" answer, and left. I said to wait by the phone because that salesperson will be calling with a better deal. Never did. Ever. Three days later my Dad cooled off on buying one, bought a pickup instead, and was glad he didn't get the Trooper. The dealership was closed 6 months later. It is that important to make every sale.

Every number you get from the salesperson, or manager is designed to make money for the dealership. Most dealerships use a variation of the foursquare method of presentation. It's meant to draw in several profit components, give the store something to talk about and something of value to give up, and still hold profit, and mostly, to confuse the customer. There is a saying in negotiation, it's not how much, but how many times. As an example, let's say you are unhappy with the trade number (shock), and you want more. The manager has already held profit to give him some room to negotiate the trade. Let's assume he is holding $2000 less than what he thinks it's worth. Instead of just giving you the $2000, he will give you maybe $300, which you say no, then $200 more, which you still say no, then totally caves in and give you another $100. Now he has given up $600 of the $2000 he was undervaluing your trade for. But more important, psychologically, you are thinking that he has already conceded three times, with each time getting smaller, so must be really towards the end of what he is going to offer you. And you are thinking that maybe next time it will be only 50 bucks, so why bother and just cave in. This happens on every trade, price, payment, and down payment. It's not how much, but how many times.

The foursquare method gives you four numbers to look at. Most dealers will present all four numbers regardless if you are paying cash, except if you have no trade. This is to get you to think about financing, just planting the seed for later. These four items are:

Price: This will be the price you got from them that brought you in, or one that the car is listed for.

Trade: This will be what they are allowing you for your trade.

Payment: If you are financing the car, they will give you various payments based on the term of the loan. They won't be accurate, and always high, because at this point they have not pulled credit. If you are leasing, it will be very similar. For instance, they will quote a 24 month payment, a 36, 48 and 60. And with that they will have $0 down, then $1000, $3000, and $6000. Everyone always wants the lowest payment with the least down, so it gets your attention to the $0 down, longest term payment. $6000 down and $900 a month doesn't usually end up being the one picked.

Down payment: Even if you said you didn't want to put any money down, they will always give you a down payment scenario. It's to scare you a bit, and something they can easily wipe out to make you feel good.

If you have done your homework, got a solid price before you came in, have a realistic value for your trade, know your credit and what interest rate you can get, and what your payment would be, you would think it would be fairly straight forward, it's not going to be. You are going to have to analyze each component for its own merit.

Hint: Do not tell them what your offers are from other dealers. Keep this information to yourself until you get a final, final number. If you reveal anything, you may be leaving money on the table (paying too much). You can tell them before you begin that you have been shopping however, and I think that would be a good tactic. Remember the old saying "Two ears and one mouth".

In negotiating, you can't just shoot from the hip, either. It's easy for someone to tell if you are lying, or the numbers are way out of whack.If you do, the manager may not want to do business with you, and you may lose the opportunity to buy there. People are people.

Before I got into the car business, I was a farmer. We needed a truck, so I headed to our local dealer to see what they had and get a price. It was a small town, and I knew the salesmen, good guys. They had a truck I liked, so I was given a price. He said it was the best he could do, wanted to keep things local, and knew me. $100 over invoice. I was paying cash, no trade.

I felt he was honest and don't believe there was anything funny about it. Of course I drove to the big city dealer 30 miles away, to keep him honest. Same truck, but they said they would like to steal a deal from the other dealer, so would give up the $100. Said I would think about it, and left. So I know I was getting the bottom price from both dealers. But before I left the big city dealers office, I grabbed a sheet of his personalized notepad, without their knowledge, and wrote a quote on it for $1000 less. The next day I brought this back to my local dealer, and after hearing the owner yell at my salesman for 20 minutes, they took that deal. There are two lessons in this. One is that every dealer is under tremendous pressure to sell cars, and I honestly believe they were losing money to keep me as a customer. Two, and most importantly, is that I lied. I have never felt good about what I did, and has stuck with me for 40 years. I started selling cars at the other one of two dealerships in that town, and was there for 9 years, and became very good friends with those salespeople. I never told them what I did, I was too embarrassed. Honesty is always your best policy.

"If I could would you". No matter how it is said, and sometimes it's very smooth, but in essence that is what negotiating is all about. No matter what you are negotiating on, the salesperson's goal is to get you to commit. If I could get that price, would you take it home today. If I could get you that payment, would you take it home today. You said if I could give you that for your trade, you said you would take it home today. Never agree you will take it home today. Just say possibly, and you won't be lying. A dealer wants to sell and deliver you a car right then, while you are emotionally involved. If you have done all your homework and feel like it's the right time, then go ahead. But if you don't, go home and truly think about it. They will try to shame you into taking the car if you make any indication that a certain concession will get you to drive it home. Don't sign anything, that is another commitment they will try to hold you to.

Once you feel you have gotten every penny, politely inform them of the numbers you have gotten from other dealers if they are less. If they are more, obviously don't. You can certainly turn the "If I could would you" right back at them. If you would sell me the car for this, I will take it right now. If you will lease the car for this, I will take it right now. If fact, if you don't you will never get your best deal.

Negotiation is an art, and a 1000 page book all in itself. The main point being the dealer is trying to hold as much as they can in every way that they can. There will come to a point that it doesn't make sense for them to sell it on your terms. When they walk you out the door at those final numbers, and any more is not there, then you know you are probably at the end. There is no reason to beat a dead horse any longer, take the deal and be happy with your new car.

Everyone's deal is different. Vehicle purchased, trade, money down, credit, way to buy. Let's look at each one of these individually, but I recommend you read each one, even if they don't apply to you. There is information in each section that you will want to know. Before we begin, let's assume a couple of things. I will cover poor credit later.

1. Every state has tax, license, transfer fees, lien fees, and others. A dealership is not going to overcharge you for these. If you really want to know, you can look up the DMV for your state, and find the fees they charge. Waste of time. Be aware that when you trade, most, but not all, states will give you a tax break on the trade value, and only charge you tax on the difference. Big

bonus for trading. If you are trading a lease, you will not get the credit, because you only paid tax on the portion you used anyway.

2. You have decent credit. A car score of 650 or more on your credit report should be enough for you to score either Tier1 or Tier 2. These will get you the best rates. Lower tiers will generally carry a higher interest rate.

Paying cash, no trade: Doesn't get any simpler than this. You basically get the best price for the vehicle you want from several dealers. There are some things to watch for, however. Dealerships will not typically include tax, title, and other state fees in their quote. These are left out to get you in with a lower quote. That's fine, just be aware. The other thing you will encounter is when you go to sign out, the dealership will charge a Doc fee (documentation fee) for doing the paperwork. It is different in all states, and governed by state law. Highest I have heard of is almost $800, so you may want to have that included in the quote you get in writing before you come in.

Paying cash, with trade: When you are trading, and comparing quotes from several dealers, the only thing you should be concerned with is difference. That is the amount of cash you'll write a check out for. Again, taxes and Doc fees will most likely not be included. I know I talked about figuring out your trade value, but here is a surefire way to find out. Take it to two dealers who buy cars. One's that don't interest you in their product. They will give you a hard number, one they will write a check out for to you. This gives you something to fall back on in the event the dealership where you are buying a car does not want your car, or are offering you way less. Consider the tax savings however. And you have something to back up a value, and appraisers do respect other appraiser's opinions.

As I mentioned in the financing portion of this book, the business manager will try to get you to keep your cash, and finance. If he does get you to do that, get the figures from him, in writing, and leave. After all the time and effort spent picking out and negotiating for a car, the customer is usually tired and just wants to get it over at this point. The dealership counts on this, that's why the finance office is the most profitable one in the dealership. You will need to verify the interest rate they are giving you if you don't pay cash, and if you intended to when you went shopping, probably didn't check with your bank or credit union.

Financing, no trade: Another fairly straight up purchase, or so you would think. If you are financing the car, you are most concerned about the payment. As I talked about in the financing portion of the book, the finance office makes their money on rate markup. May not seem much a month, but could cost you hundreds if not thousands over time. Typically, at the time of negotiation with the sales desk, they will quote you a payment that you will close on, with the credit disclaimer that if you are not a top tier, your payment might be higher. Most dealerships will mark up the rate 2 to 3 percent from their buy rate. Keep in mind, dealerships are not holding the loan. They are cashing out of it with a lender, who will send them the money when the contract is funded by the lender. If you have, and I hope at this point you have, done your homework and gotten a good payment, the finance office may try to switch the term with you, as in make it longer to lower your payment. If they do, they may be able to bump the rate because you are not prepared for this scenario, and it will cost you a lot more interest in the long run. When you finally do sign the contract, make sure the interest rate, term, selling price, and fees are right. Remember, you closed on a payment. There is a chance that they got a better buy rate than disclosed, if they disclosed it, and raised the price of the car to get you the same payment.

Financing with trade: The biggest calculation that customers and salespeople combined had a problem figuring out is when it comes to trade payoffs. Many times an inaccurate payoff quote causes a mistake in the paperwork, and you will be asked to resign. They have you sign a paper that says you will come back in if the information is incorrect. You don't have to, and can return the car at this point if something looks fishy. One scenario may be that you owed $500 more than you thought, and the payment goes up like you owed $1000. More profit for the store. Again, a simple calculation on your phone could tell you how much it should be. What if you owe more than what the car is worth. A very, very common theme. That amount over what you owe is added to the amount of the loan, and in essence you are making payments on the new car, and on the old one too. Don't be afraid to ask questions, take notes, research on your phone in front of them. They can be very intimidating and try to rush you into making a decision. The slower you make the process at this stage, the more cool headed you will be, and make more informed decisions.

Leasing, no trade: You are renting the car for a specified period of time and miles, and your only decision will be how much money down, and what's the payment. Most times lease payments are quoted without tax and license included. One, it makes the payment lower, and two, every state charges differently. Some states require the dealership to pay all the fees up front, some states charge the tax monthly. So when you request the quote, Make sure you are comparing apples to apples. The down payment on a lease is call cap cost reduction. So if you are putting money down, whatever you put down lowers the monthly payment. A lot of times customers are drawn in by an advertised lease with money down. In reality, the money down is actually lowering the lease payment. For example, let's say you come in for a $199 a month lease for 36 months. The down payment, outside of taxes and fees is $1999 cash. A dealership will never advertise tax and fees either down or in the payment, simply because sales usually cross state lines, and your tax rate might be different, or you may have a trade that changes things. Back to the example, if you take the $1999, and translate that into 36 months of payments, it would add $55.52 a month to the payment, for a total payment of $254.52 with no money down. Just keep that in mind when comparing leases, and realistically, why would you put any money down on a lease. They come with Gap insurance (to protect you if total the car and it's worth less than you owe), and it's just a payment, usually with a low interest rate.

The biggest thing to watch for when going into the finance office to sign out on a lease is if they try to switch the term or miles contracted for. They do this to increase the money factor to try and make some money or the residual, again to make more money. Make sure that you check the quoted rate from the agreed upon paperwork from the sales desk to the changed quote from the finance office to make sure they are the same, and if not, an explanation why. Again, these rates can and should be negotiated.

Lease, with trade: All the above scenarios apply, with the exception now your trade becomes cap cost reduction. Your car has a cash value (ACV) so it's just like having a stack of cash on the desk you are giving them on the lease, minus anything you owe, which will decrease your payment. In the event you owe more than its value, it's like having an IOU instead, and they will add it to the contract, which will increase your payment. In many states, you can get cash back out of your trade. This means the dealership will write you out a check for any amount up to the ACV, but then you get no payment benefit for that amount. Trades also lower your tax bill in most states just like a retail trade, which is a benefit, but you need to ask when negotiating with the desk if it applies. Once you use your trade equity on a lease, that money is gone. There will not be any money coming back to you at the end. I have heard it hundreds of times that someone used a $10000 trade on a lease, got some killer payments, then when the lease was up, came back in to find that now they have no equity for the next lease, and the payments on a similar car they originally bought is now $300 a month higher. There are only 4 things to watch for on your lease if you trade. Selling price, trade in amount, money factor (interest rate), and residual (value at end of lease). If you change any of the things like term or miles, make sure you are comfortable that the rates or something else weren't changed.

Let's talk about the people you will work with:

Salesperson: A salesperson is hired and trained to be your best friend, and there is nothing wrong with that. They are there to help you, but also don't make money unless they sell something. It is in their best interest to make you happy, because happy people buy. A lot of times, a salesperson will side with the customer, and coach them on how to buy a car from there, and their manager. Some of this may be true, and some of it may be a sales technique. If you understand the relationship you have with them, and understand the buying process, it will be very apparent. You can, and should, use the fact that they don't get paid to help you buy a car. It can be as simple as "I really want to buy a car from you, but I need your help to get the deal I want". Believe me, if they sense it might help them sell a car, they will work the manager for you with fervor.

Manager: A manager's main job is to control the sale, and make money for the store. That is how they get paid, off the departments profit. They didn't get their job because they weren't good at what they do, they are. Some are gruff, some are bullies, some are smooth, all are just people doing their job. You will get nowhere with a manager by playing tough or being rude. Their financial commitment in each deal is less than a salesperson's, simply because of volume, so are more apt to dig their feet in when confronted or angered. You are much better off if you can finalize a deal with the salesperson only, but keep in mind that you will most likely have to talk to a manager to get the absolute final number. The most likely scenario you will encounter is that you get what is told a final number from the salesperson, take it or leave it. And if you don't, which I recommend, is to leave. Either that salesperson will be instructed to call you back with a better deal, or the manager themselves will call you back. Either way, you have now won.

Business Manager (finance guy): In most stores, these are the most highly paid, highly skilled and smoothest employees. They are good at taking money out of your pocket, and putting it into theirs. With leases, you have to go with the dealership, but you can finance anywhere you get the best rate. This department also sells service contracts (warranties), gap insurance, paint protection, wheel and tire coverage, excessive wear and tear, among other things. I will talk about those in more detail later. These folks are trained to build instant rapport, tell lots of stories before they get to selling, and make you feel as comfy as a kitten. There is usually friction between the sales department and the finance department too, as they try to get their money too. Don't be afraid, no matter how much they try to get you to sign, that you can politely get everything in writing, and walk out. Again, a cool head will make much better decisions.

As I said before, there is no reason why it can't be a win/win for both parties. You need to save money (unless you are mega rich then who cares), and the dealership needs to make a profit. There is always a middle ground that can and should be reached. Don't try to squeeze out every penny, it's not worth living your life that way. Accept that they may make a few hundred bucks on you and move on. You do it every day where you shop for food, clothes, furniture and everything else you buy. And you affecting someone's income. Whether you work hourly or get a salary, I'm pretty sure no one is hitting you up every day to work for less. It boils down to this in negotiating. BE FAIR.

CHAPTER 8
WARRANTIES

There are basically two kinds of warranties. New car warranties that are backed by the manufacturer of the vehicle, and used car warranties, commonly called extended service contracts, that can be backed by a manufacturer or a third party. They have different coverages depending on what kind of car you are buying. They are designed to give you peace of mind. They are also like car and home insurance, and health insurance, that if you never use them, you have wasted your money. If you do use them, they may be the best thing you ever did.

No matter new or used, to keep a warranty in effect, you must maintain the vehicle according to the maintenance schedules recommended by the manufacturer, which will be found in the owner's manual.

New Car warranties: A new car warranty is the number one reason that people will purchase a new car instead of a used one. Each manufacturer has different terms, coverages, and mileage limits. Anywhere from lifetime powertrain warranty, five year bumper to bumper, and twelve year rust protection, and so forth. The warranty coverage is listed on the Monroney sticker, and also all over the internet. They come at no cost when you purchase a new car. What you are going to run into when you are doing the paperwork in the finance office, you will be presented an opportunity to purchase an extended warranty, which will take effect when the manufacturer's warranty has expired.

If you are leasing, there is no way I would purchase an extended service contract. You may be buying the car at the end of term, and you can make your decision then, no matter how much they try to tell you that you will save a bunch by getting it at time of leasing. That is simply not true.

Even if you are paying cash or financing, and plan on keeping the car forever, you can still purchase a warranty if you really want one before the manufacturer's warranty expires. At that point you will have a much better idea three or four years down the road if you still plan on keeping the car.

I have purchased many new cars, and have never purchased one. On the used cars I have purchased, some I wanted the protection, others not so much.

Used car warranties: You may be purchasing a used car with some manufacturer warranty left on it. That is one of the appeals of buying a rental car, or short term leased car. The manufacturer warranty stays with the car no matter who owns it, and does not cost anything. The manufacturer warranty starts the day it is originally purchased, and as covered above, is different terms depending on what kind of car it is. The original service date is on a history report, like Carfax, and the report usually gives you the coverage that applies, and how much coverage you have left. This is important to know, because you will need this information in deciding on whether to purchase an extended service contract. Again, as stated above, you may purchase the extended warranty at any time before the new car warranty is up, for a better price than if it has expired. Once the original warranty has expired, service contracts become more expensive, for obvious reasons.

Let's face facts. Some cars are more reliable than others. I hope that in doing you research, reliability is one of the factors in choosing what kind of car to buy. In spite of that, I have worked at luxury brand dealerships, and even knowing that a car has a terrible reliability history, someone still wants the car because it looks good on them. And that's ok. Just be aware of what you are getting and for what reasons. I saw those same people many times in the service department. There are numerous ratings you can find on the internet, Consumer Reports being one of the better ones.

You have chosen your used car, negotiated a good deal, now are ready to sign out. The service contract will be presented at this time. There are numerous lengths, mileages, coverages, and deductibles to choose from. The finance person will make their recommendation, and go over how not having one will cost you thousands in repairs. I have always thought it funny that your salesperson will spend hours convincing you that what you are buying is a great dependable car, then the finance person will contradict the whole thing by saying it is sure to break down.

Prices vary by make. Understandable since different vehicles have different repair histories. That hot luxury car with the poor repair record will cost you the most to warranty. The reason is because of the high cost of repair. An extended warranty company makes money by taking more money in from selling their warranty, than shelling out in repairs. Each brand and car is calculated by that measurement.

The salesperson during the trade appraisal is taught to inquire if you have an extended service contract on your car. He will state that you will get a higher appraisal because it increases the chance that you have maintained it better. It also sets you up for the finance person if you feel that was the case. It's not. Your trade stands on its own merit. It is worth what it's worth, and needs what it needs. The only time it may make a difference, is that if something major needed to be replaced, and you had an existing warranty in effect that would cover it, it could be fixed for free. But you probably would have had it repaired before you came in anyway.

One of the pitches you will hear is that the warranty will never be priced as low as on the day you purchase your car. That may or not be true, again depending on the running repair history. You may and can buy an extended contract from a dealer or outside vender at any time.

Another thing you will hear, is that you can put it into the financing right now, and pay for it monthly instead of all at one time. This is true except you will also be paying interest on the amount, and it will cost you more in the long run. If you don't have the cash, most dealers offer to sell service contracts on a credit card, thereby doing the same thing, and you can decide at any time.

I always put my two cents in also when speaking with customers. My pitch was that I would never sell a car to a relative or friend unless they also got a warranty. "I don't want them to call me back when they have a problem" is what I would say.

The last scare tactic you will hear is what if you don't have the money to fix your car if something goes wrong. Again, a credit card can be used for that. And the final one is that the bank that is giving you the loan would be more comfortable if you had a warranty in place. That may be somewhat true if you have terrible credit and no ability to pay, but on the other hand, they would rather have you owe less on the car in case they repossess, instead of a two or three thousand dollar warranty.

Your chance of ever getting back what you paid for the warranty in repairs is against you. Extended service contracts use the day that the car was originally put into service as their start date, but the coverage of the extended warranty does not start until the original manufacturer's warranty has expired. If you should decide to cancel the warranty before it is up, you will get a prorated return. It would shock you how little you get back in those cases.

Most dealerships will offer 30 to 60 day warranties, which come with the car. Some are sold as is, but a reputable dealership will address any issues as they come up in those cases. These warranties give you the chance to use the car for a while to see if something comes up. But I recommend you have had a certified mechanic inspect the car before you buy it. They usually cover very little, mostly the major stuff, so pay close attention to make everything works before you sign for the car. In case it does need something, the dealership will provide a We Owe form, which is an IOU for the repair. This is perfectly legit.

You may be one of the unlucky ones and get a car that needs lots of repairs. You can narrow that risk down significantly by researching the make and model's reliability, and having your third-party mechanic give it a once over. Or if peace of mind helps you sleep at night, you just might consider it.

Lastly, don't be afraid to hurt the finance person's feelings, after all the rapport they have built up. Your decision whether to purchase one or not should be decided before you get to the dealership, and certainly before you enter the finance office to sign out. That way, a simple but firm no will suffice, and you can move on to other products that will be presented.

CHAPTER 9
DEALER ADD ONS

We have talked a bit about two of the dealer add ons, financing and extended service contracts. There are plenty more. You may find when you arrive at the dealership after doing your research, and negotiated the best price over the internet, that the car you are interested in has what is called an addendum sticker attached to it. On it are listed items installed on the vehicle which raises the price. Unless these items were mentioned in the internet negotiation, they will expect you to pay for them if you want that car. It could be anything from floor mats for $120, to a list of items totaling $5000. These items may or not be installed. Sometimes the dealer will put things up like paint protection for $495, and only doing it at the time of sale, not before.

The first thing you are going to want to do is to determine if they in fact have been installed. Then you are going to have to determine their worth to you. Many items are not worth getting, and the dealer has a huge profit built into them. They may not make much on the car, but they certainly do on the add ons.

If they have already been done, then you have to do your research to see if they have any value to you. If they don't, then ask if they can be removed, because they have no value to you and would like them to be removed. If you do see value, then you will need to negotiate each item you want. Keep this negotiation separate from the price of the car, which you have already determined.

Here are some of the common ones, and how much profit the dealer makes on each one.

Gap insurance: Already included in leases, this covers the difference on what you owe on the car, to what an insurance company will pay if the car gets totaled. Worthless if you pay cash, and worth very little if you finance. How many cars have you totaled in your lifetime? Dealer profit $300 - $400.

Lease wear and tear: This is nice to have if you are tough on your car and are leasing. It covers a wide variety of mishaps that you would be charged for upon returning the vehicle, including losing an expensive key. Dealer profit $200-$400.

Paint protection: Basically, a wax job. Dealer profit $300-$500.

Fabric protection: Again, a can of Scotchguard. Dealer profit $300-$400.

Pin striping: $10 for the tape, $25 to put it on. Dealer profit $100- 300.

Vin etching: In the glass for theft. Besides marked parts on the car, and anti-theft systems and keys, this probably rates up there with the most worthless. Dealer profit $100-$200

Rustproofing: Not needed anymore, and not sold much. Big profit for dealer $700-900.

Undercoating: Another thing of the past. Dealer profit $500-700.

Car alarm: There are many places that install this for much less. Dealer profit $600- $900.

Lojack: GPS in case your car gets stolen. Lots of cars have this ability already built in. You might find that your car already has it, and they are still trying to sell you one. Dealer profit $500-$700.

ADM: Additional Dealer Markup. Mostly used when a car is hard to get.

It is all dealer profit. Sky's the limit.

Remote starter: Very handy to have. If you have it put on aftermarket, it just might void the manufacturer's warranty. If you want it, you should be able to negotiate it down some. Dealer profit $ 200-$400.

Wheel package: Upgraded wheels put on by the dealer. Dealer profit $500-$1000.

Spoiler: Made to enhance the look, if you like that look. Many accessories are installed by the manufacturer, such as spoilers. They will always cost less than the dealer installing it, simply because of labor cost, and huge volume discounts. Dealer profit $150-$300.

Window tinting: Much cheaper at an outside vender. Dealer profit $300-$500.

Nitrogen in tires: Keeps the air in the tires longer, but you may have a hard time finding places to refill. Regular air is free. Dealer profit $75-$150.

Trailer hitch: Many places install these for less. Dealer profit $300- $1000.

Bed liners: Same as above. Dealer profit $200-$300.

Running boards: Again, many places specialize in installing aftermarket accessories. They are very competitive in their pricing. Dealer profit $400-$700.

License plate brackets, valve stem caps, mirror covers, colored grills, and many more are just some of the items you will commonly find as the dealer tries to build more profit.

Once you have determined any items that have value to you, or if they have been installed, you can start to negotiate them using the dealer profit projections above. The sales desk will approach parts and service for a price break if they can't get it from the customer. Those two departments do not want a charge back, or returning the item to inventory. Let the three of them duke it out to see what they can come up with. Finally, if you feel that you are just being taken advantage of, then it's time to walk. I personally have thrown in many add ons just to get rid of the car. Cars are always harder to sell with items added to them, and you should know that they will have absolutely no resale value when it comes time to trade. One dealership I worked for, every pickup that came in with a topper, and there were a lot of them, had the topper removed and thrown out back in a pile. Anyone that wanted one in town could just come and get them for free. These are the same toppers that someone who bought the truck paid over a thousand dollars for a few years previous.

If you are looking at buying a new car, they also have add ons from the manufacturer listed on the Monroney sticker (this is what the new car sticker is called). You do not have to negotiate these items as they are included in the MSRP, of which you have already done.

Finally, buying add on items is a personal choice, but for the most part many of these items have no value, cost too much, and can be done for much less outside of the dealership.

Case in point. You see these trucks with the monster tires and rims, all decked out with chrome, special paint, costing thousands to do. They are worth less than the same truck with original equipment. The resale market for them is very small, and most people will shy away from these monsters because they are not going to be seen dead in one.

CHAPTER 10
SERVICE AND PARTS

Fact or fiction: Dealerships charge more for getting service or buying parts there. Fact. There are a few reasons why this is so. They have a captive audience for getting warranty work done on your vehicle. A franchised dealer is the only place you can have warranty work done and get it paid for. Some exceptions apply in case of emergencies, but are handled case by case. Another reason is the investment in tools and training for working on specific makes of vehicles. They are required to have expensive software, special tools, and highly trained technicians. It costs them more per hour than other shops. They sell OEM parts (Original Equipment Manufacturer) parts and install them. These parts cost more than aftermarket parts. And the manufacturer requires that the facility is up to standards. Better coffee too.

Should you go to the dealership to have your car repaired. That depends.

Manufacturer warranty: To get covered repairs, you'll have to go to the dealer. This is not bad, this is good. You will most likely be working with a service advisor for that make. Depending on what you purchase, you may see them a lot, or never meet them. This person gets paid commission on what they sell. It's called upselling. You may come in for a covered repair, and they will recommend other items you may want done, even if not recommended by the manufacturer at that time. They are judged and paid by hours per RO (Repair order). Just coming in for an oil change, and turning down the tire rotation, tranny flush, and wheel balancing works against them the same as not taking things in the finance office. Goes against their average. These people are some of the best salespeople in the dealership, make very good money, and use the soft scare tactic to get you to buy things. "You want your family safe, don't you" is a very common one. Another is "I feel concerned to let you drive your car home in the condition it is in." Unless required by the manufacturer for warranty purposes, stick with the recommended manufacturer recommendations, out of the owner's manual, and not a printed one that the dealer made.

Extended service contract: The same scenario applies from the new car warranty, but in this case, you may be informed it is not a covered repair, has a deductible to pay, or needs to be pre-authorized. You may even need to pay for the repair, and later submit the bill to the warranty company for reimbursement. Extended warranties may be issued by the manufacturer, insurance companies, or companies set up to administer them. You don't really have to go back to the original dealer for them to pay for repairs, but it usually goes much smoother if you go back to the place that sold it to you.

Customer pay: This is the biggest profit generator for the service and parts department. New car and used car warranties have a set labor rate that the dealership can get reimbursed for. It is always lower than customer pay, which is when someone is not covered by a warranty. Although they do have to be somewhat competitive, they count on the relationship that was built up during the warranty coverage period you have with the service advisor, and use that trust to keep you coming back. People are creatures of habit. We all like to go back to the same restaurants, the same gas stations, and the same stores we are comfortable with. Same holds true for getting your car fixed. Can you get service for less somewhere else? Sure. You can go to any quick lube and get an oil change for $15 bucks, and pay double that at a dealer. You need to decide what works for you. Most dealers will honor competitor coupons, and run specials all the time.

Having your car serviced really isn't any different than buying one. You need to do your research on what needs to be done, how much it is going to cost, and where you want to go to have it done. There is value in having a factory trained technician work on your car, and you may find that a used car you bought from dealer A is not a dealer for that make of car, and you may want to go to the dealer that is.

In the end, just be aware that your service advisor is a salesperson, and will employ may tactics to upsell profit items for the dealership. Even though they may not have as much profit to work with, if you can justify a better price somewhere else, most likely they will want your business and match or beat it.

CHAPTER 11
HOW MUCH DO SALESPEOPLE MAKE

No book on buying a car would be complete without you being aware how much a salesperson makes by selling cars for a living. Every dealership pays with variation on the same old theme. You are paid on what you produce. They all have their own pay plans, and we will focus on just the commission, salary, and bonus parts of the income. We will leave out all the benefits like 401K, health insurance, demo's, and the like.

For the record, I have worked in 4 dealerships in my 28 years, and have trained, coached, hired, and fired hundreds of salespeople. I have had people make $18,000 a year, and some that make $250,000 a year. The only thing that separates them is their motivation, skill level, and a bit of luck. Being in the right place at the right time. Some dealerships just have more traffic, or a better product, so a salesperson working there would make more.

The most common way of paying a salesperson is commission. They are paid on the gross profit of the vehicle, expressed as a percentage. Example: Let's say you are paid 25% of up front gross on every used car you sell. You sell a car and gross $2000, you are then paid $500 commission. Not bad. However, most stores have what they call a pack, which is what the store gets for taking the risk and reconditioning the cars, and the pack can range anywhere for a few hundred dollars to more than a thousand. This comes right off the gross. That $2000 gross becomes $1500 if the pack is $500, then the commission would be paid off the $1500, or $375, $125 less in the salespersons pocket. There is a lot of incentive for getting gross.

There are also bonus programs for hitting sales targets. A common one is $500 for hitting 8 cars in a month, $800 more for hitting 12 cars, $1000 more for hitting 15 and so forth. Getting gross and selling volume is key to making a good living. Some other things pay spiffs, like getting a warranty, good CSI (customer satisfaction index), and accessories. They are usually not much.

Some stores pay on the back end too, which is the money that the finance department makes. The theory here is that if the salesperson gets paid from finance, they will do a better job of endorsing their products. It does help, but profit suffers from the extra pay, and the salesperson generally doesn't have or care to have that much control over that office.

New cars are usually on the same plan, but you can seldom hold gross on new, so typically salespeople are paid a flat commission anywhere from $50 to $500, depending on brand, volume, and age of vehicle. They do however count towards bonus levels, to encourage sales of new vehicles too. Most salespeople would much rather sell used vehicles. Bigger gross, easier to deliver, usually no surveys, and less competition because used cars are more one of a kind.

Commissioned salespeople fall under the minimum wage laws, and their draw or base salary covers the hours they are supposed to work. Let's see how two different salespeople make a living.

Salesperson A is new. He starts out with a draw of $1500, and his commissions are applied to that, and anything over at the end of the month he gets. He has already figured out that it's a volume game, but with no former customers or referrals, has to rely on floor traffic, phone calls, and a few internet leads. The manager is on his case every day to sell cars. At the end of the month, he has sold 4 used cars, and 4 new cars. The national average is 12 cars a month for salespeople, taking into consideration new and seasoned professionals. His used cars netted him $375 each in commission, and all his new were mini's (minimum commission). He hit the bonus for 8 cars for $500. He has no surveys returned yet, and didn't endorse any warranties. So here I what he earned for the month.

4 X $375 = $1500 for used cars sold

4 X $100 = $400   for new cars sold

8 car bonus = $500

Total commission for the month= $2400

If he continues to sell cars like this, he will earn $28,800 a year. This is a job which usually requires at least 50 hours a week, some places open on Sunday, always work Saturdays and nights. That's $9.60 an hour. But at least it's a clean job. Would you work for this?

Now let's look at salesperson B. She has put in the work, and has been on the job for 10 years. She is well liked, knows her job, and has built a nice repeat and referral business. They both work in the same dealership. Because of her work, she gets more of the internet leads, and given more house deals because the managers will know that the people will be taken care of. Her month looks like this.

8 X $500 = $4000 for used cars sold

8 X $200 = $1600 for new cars sold

16 car bonus = $2300

Survey and warranty bonus = $250

Total commission for the month = $8150

She gets more per car in gross because of her repeat business, and sells more cars too. Her yearly income is $97,800, or $32.60 an hour.

This is a very realistic look at how different salespeople perform. You will never know who you get when you are dealing on the internet, phone, or walk in the door. Not sure how you feel about stereotypes, but the low volume salesperson is sometimes new, and sometimes the old dude with the plaid jacket and gold chains. The high performer is usually very personable, easy to be with, and becomes your best friend. All I can say is that car salespeople work hard for their money. There are plenty of lazy ones too, but that is in every profession, and generally they are weeded out over time.

The one unfortunate part of the car business, is that earning power has not increased in the 28 years that I have been in the business. Salespeople and managers were making the same then as they are now. What used to be a very good, well paying, job that was easy to hire for, is now a mediocre job which it's tough to get anyone to do.

Most of the salespeople you will deal with average in the $30,000 to $40,000 a year bracket. They work hard for their money, put in long hours, deal with lots of drama, and deal with a lot of stress. There is a lot of turnover in this business, and the reputation that goes along with selling cars, undeservedly so, doesn't help them feel good about what they do. A kind word and a smile will definitely help in your quest to save money. They will work very hard for you when given a reason to.

CHAPTER 12
BAD CREDIT

It happens to the best of us. The reason I ended up selling cars was I had terrible credit, went into buy a van for cleaning carpets, and couldn't get financed. I got a job instead. Things happen that hurts your credit, some you can help, and some you can't. If the person helping you to get a loan is made aware of a situation that hurt your credit through no fault of your own, that story might possibly help getting the lending institution to say yes. If you do have bad credit, have a story to back up why.

Unfortunately, bad credit is taken advantage of in the industry. There are buy here pay here lots, and special finance departments set up in dealerships. You will see lots of advertising for this business, come on in, we will get you done. Bad credit, no credit, no problem. The industry knows they have the upper hand, because these people are desperate, and will do just about anything to get a car. If you do have bad credit, here are some things to watch out for, and the reasons that are behind them.

Buy here pay here lots. These can be one person lots, or franchised lots. You pay way more for the vehicle than it's worth, and make payments directly to them either weekly or monthly. Sometimes they install a disabling or tracking devise on the car should you stop paying. I have seen them sell $1000 cars for over $5000, and people will pay because they need a car. Of course, the interest rate charged is extremely high. Unfortunately, this is the only way for some folks to be able to get a vehicle, so they do serve a purpose.

Dealerships that have a special finance department aren't so brutal. Sure, it will cost you more interest, sometimes much more, and you can only select from a small selection of cars. This is because the lenders that they use have strict book to value rules, to protect them from default. The last thing anyone wants to do is repossess the car. That's why a salesperson will bring up ability to pay as one of the first qualifying questions asked. They want to know if you need special financing, because that will limit the type of cars to show you.

A salesperson loves a Get Me Done (as it's called in the business). They know that they can pretty much sell them anything on the lot, for any price, if they can "Get them done". It doesn't take much for selling skills, the close ratio is high, but actually delivering a vehicle is low, because usually these people have been turned down all over, sometimes for good reason. They call sending it to the lender "throwing it against the wall", to see if a lender bites. If it does get approved, there is usually a lot of profit in it for the dealer because these people don't negotiate because they are coming from a position of weakness.

If you are in that situation, let me offer this. I would try getting a loan from a relative, a credit union where you bank, or maybe someone to co-sign the loan for you. If you know you can buy, you will have a much better selection of vehicles which to choose from, and you will save thousands in interest charges. You need to work this out before you step on a car lot. If you don't, just the thought of you getting a car, any car, may blind you to the fact that you are paying too much, and will just keep you in a situation where you still struggle to make the payments, and keep you in that same situation.

If having bad credit is your situation, then before you set foot on a car lot to buy a car, you should start rebuilding your credit before you get there. Here are some steps you can take to improve your chances of getting a decent loan.

1. Pull your credit report to see where you stand. There are three major credit reporting agencies, all doing very much the same thing. They are Experian, Equifax, and Transunion. You can correct any mistakes there may be, or pay any collections or liens you might have open that you forgot about. I have seen some as low as a few bucks that are hurting someone's score.

2. Join a Credit Union. If you can find one that is connected to your occupation, like Teachers, Police Officers, Firemen, you should choose that one. If you don't, then any one will be fine. As a member, they want to help you. Your chances improve greatly of getting a loan from them.

3. Make sure you don't pay your bills late. If you are behind, catch up. I have seen customers that are behind six months on their car loans, and figure that getting a new one, they will get the old loan paid and start over. Doesn't work that way.

4. Like we talked about previously, line up a co-signer. It has to be someone with good credit however. Two bad scores do not make a good one.

5. Apply for a secured credit card if you have no credit. A credit union will usually be a good place to get one. It is a card that is connected to an account that you place money in, usually up to $500. That then becomes your limit on how much you can charge on the card. If you don't have funds in the account, you can't charge anything.

6. Another thing would to apply for store cards, like Sears or Penny's, or gas cards. They will not boost your score as much as the major Visa and MasterCard, but it will show some history.

7. Get a personal loan. The idea is getting some kind of loan that reports to the credit bureaus, to show that you are responsible in making payments. If you are getting or have student loans, make sure you are keeping up with those payments as well.

8. Time on your job. This is a big one for getting a loan. The longer you are on the same job, or at least the same line of work, it will make a big difference to the lender.

Someone who job hops will be perceived as not very dependable, and most likely to have a period with no income, and no ability to pay.

9. Make sure you take care of your obligations. Don't ignore the things you are responsible for. When a bill comes in the mail, pay it. Pay your rent or house payment on time. Don't let things pile up. If you need help, borrow from a relative, or get a personal loan to clean everything up and get a fresh start.

10. Leave old debt on your report if it is paid off. The longer the history you can show, the better.

11. Consolidate credit cards into one or two, and leave the others showing paid. This will tell the lender you have unused credit. They don't like to see someone maxed out on credit. That flags a default.

FINAL THOUGHTS

20 years ago, the internet was going to do away with how the automobile business was structured. No more dealers, everything would be sold online and delivered direct to the customer from the manufacturer. No need for salespeople, managers, and others involved with the retailing of cars. There would be service centers that would pick up your vehicle or service it at your location. There was going to be a lot of changes. Guess what, none of the predictions happened.

What did happen was positive for the consumer and the dealer. There was more competition, which is good for the consumer. There was more full disclosure, which is good for dealerships to get rid of the bad eggs in the business that was giving it a black eye. People still want to try before they buy, and that is the beauty of retail stores. Hey, I order a lot online and have it delivered, but I still like going to a store and actually seeing and touching, what I want to buy.

There are changes in the auto business, positive ones, that the dealers themselves want to see. Finance departments have come under enormous scrutiny, as a result, have limited the markup allowed on loans (called finance reserve), have gone to a menu based selling structure where everything is disclosed, and have gone to enormous lengths to provide privacy and security to customers.

I have many friends in the auto business, lifelong friends, who still depend on selling cars as their living. Even though I am retired and don't depend on that income anymore, the last thing I want to do is affect their income. I truly believe there needs to be some changes in the way dealership personnel, especially commissioned ones, are paid. It is extremely stressful work, and the way salespeople are compensated creates a win/lose situation when dealing with clients. A salespersons job is on the line every day, every sale, every customer. I really don't think it can sustain itself in this way. Hence the wage stagnation since the 80's.

I certainly don't have the solution. The system itself is trying various alternatives to see if something works. One price, manufacturer stores, big box retailer buying programs, used car superstores, and online buying services just to name a few. Dealership groups have gone a long way to standardize the process over many stores, like the experience you have going into a fast food franchise. For now, we need to work with what we have.

I hope that in presenting this information you become a much better informed buyer, and make the buying process easier for you and the salesperson. I can guarantee that if you use this information in a logical, systematic, and non-emotional way, you will save well over a thousand dollars on your purchase, possibly two or three. Good luck on getting the deal you want, and thank you for your interest in this book.

Burl Johnson

Made in the USA
Lexington, KY
09 July 2017